Distribution and Logistics

Dr.V.V.L.N. Sastry

Submitted in partial fulfillment for meeting one of the

Phase II requirements

For the award of the degree of Post Doctorate in Economics

Atlantic International University, USA.

22nd November 2020

BRIGHT & YOUNG PUBLISHERS

Mumbai

©Copyright Author

All rights reserved. No part of this book may be reproduced, stored in a retrieval system, or transmitted, in any form by any means, electronic, mechanical, magnetic, optical, chemical, manual, photo copying, recording or otherwise, without the prior written consent of its writer.

Publishing year: December-2020

Price:

E-Book 5 USD

Printed book – 10 USD

The opinions/contents expressed in this book are solely of the author and do not represent the opinions/standings/ thoughts of Bright & Young publishers.

Distribution and Logistics

Bright & Young Publishers

BRIGHT & YOUNG PUBLISHERS

ABOUT THE AUTHOR

Dr.V.V.L.N. Sastry holds M.B.A (USA), LL.M (UK), ACMA (India), FCMA, CGMA (CIMA, UK), M.Sc. in Information Systems and Management from University of Roehampton, Ph.D. in Banking, Ph.D. in Computer Science, Ph. D in Financial Management, D.B.A from Calwest, and Ph.D. in Criminal Law and Public Policy from Walden University, U.S.A. Sastry brings over 20 years of experience in the banking, investment banking, software industry and law. He is the author of more than 1000 published articles on varied subjects in the areas of IT, Banking, Finance, Economics and Law. He also has authored several books in the said fields. Rated among the top researchers in the worldwide applied solutions, his research contributions are well received across the world.

ABOUT THE BOOK

In supply chain management, distribution is the procedure of making a product or service accessible for the customer or commercial user who wants it (Brandimarte & Zotteri, 2007). On the other hand, logistics is the administration of the movement of products between the point of source and the point of consumption so as to meet necessities of clients or businesses (Brandimarte & Zotteri, 2007). Thus, they are vital processes in the supply chain management. Therefore, to understand distribution and logistics well, we are required to critically examine some concepts that will make us understand them better. These concepts are: logistics, logistics complement, cargo, cargo airline, cargo sampling, cargo scanning and delivery, freight company, freight transport association, standard carrier alpha code and document automation, freight claim, logistics automation and performance based logistics, distribution(business) and agricultural marketing, all commodity volume, import and export, and incoterms.

Table of Contents

Introduction 1

Logistics 3

Logistics complement 6

cargo 9

Transportation Types 10

    Marine 10

    Air 10

    Train 11

    Road 11

Cargo airline, Cargo sampling, Cargo scanning and delivery 13

Freight company, Freight transport Association, Standard Carrier Alpha Code and Document automation 15

    Freight companies 15

    Freight transport Association 17

    Standard Carrier Alpha Code 17

    Document automation 18

Freight claim, Logistics automation and Performance-based logistics 19

    Freight Claim 19

    Logistics automation 20

    Performance-based logistics 21

Distribution (business) and Agricultural marketing 22

    Distribution 22

    Agricultural marketing 24

All-commodity volume **26**

Import and export **29**

    Import 29

    Export 30

Incoterms **32**

Questions **35**

References **46**

Introduction

In supply chain management, distribution is the procedure of making a product or service accessible for the customer or commercial user who wants it (Brandimarte & Zotteri, 2007). On the other hand, logistics is the administration of the movement of products between the point of source and the point of consumption so as to meet necessities of clients or businesses (Brandimarte & Zotteri, 2007). Thus, they are vital processes in the supply chain management. Therefore, to understand distribution and logistics well, we require to critically examining lengthily some concepts that will make us understand them better. These concepts are: logistics, logistics complement, cargo, cargo airline, cargo sampling, cargo scanning and delivery, freight company, freight transport association, standard carrier alpha code and document automation, freight claim, logistics automation and performance based logistics, distribution(business) and agricultural marketing, all commodity volume, import and export, and incoterms.

Logistics

Logistics is the organization of the movement of products between the point of consumption and the point of origin so as to meet some necessities, for instance, of consumers or companies (Brandimarte & Zotteri, 2007). In logistics, the resources administered can consist of physical substances, for example foodstuff, resources, animals, apparatus and fluids, in addition to immaterial substances, for instance time, data, particles, and energy. For the physical substances, the logistics habitually includes the incorporation of information movement, warehousing, manufacture, packaging, inventory, carriage, material management, and repeatedly security.

Inbound logistics is one of the principal procedures of logistics, focusing on buying and organizing the inbound flow of resources, parts, and/or completed portfolio from dealers to manufacturing or assembly plants, warehouses, or merchandising stores (Bowersox, David & Bixby, 2002). On the other hand, outbound logistics is the procedure associated to the storing and flow of the end good and the associated data movements from the end of the manufacturing line to the final consumer.

Provided the services executed by logisticians, the key disciplines of logistics can get subdivided into the following: procurement logistics, production logistics, distribution logistics, after-sales logistics, disposal logistics, reverse logistics, green logistics, global logistics, domestics logistics and Concierge Service RAM logistics.

There are different types of logistics such as military logistics where the logistics officer manages how and when to transport resources to the places they are required. On the other hand, business logistics integrates all industry sectors and purposes to manage the completion of project life cycles, supply chains, and subsequent competences.

Basically, there are two diverse forms of logistics: one enhances a stable movement of resources through a network of transportation links and storing nodes, but the other synchronizes a sequence of materials to accomplish some task.

Logistics complement

Handling systems consist of: stacker handlers, trans-pallet handlers, and bilateral handlers, counterweight handler, among others while the storage systems consist of: stack stocking, cell racks, beam racks and gravity racks (Brandimarte & Zotteri, 2007). On the other hand, order processing is a progressive procedure encompassing: processing withdrawal list, picking which is discriminatory elimination of substances from packing unit), sorting which is bringing together substances based on terminus, package establishment which includes weighting, labeling and packing, and order merging which includes gathering packages into packing units for transport, control and bill of lading.

Cargo, which is the products being transported, can get transported by a range of transportation methods and gets prearranged in dissimilar shipment kinds (Bowersox, David & Bixby, 2002). Unit loads are frequently amassed into advanced identical units for instance ISO containers, exchange bulks or semi-trailers. Particularly for very long distances, product transport probably profit from utilizing diverse transport methods: multimodal transportation, intermodal transportation and mutual transport. Machinists concerned in transportation encompasses: all train, road trucks, boats, aircrafts corporations, carriers, cargo forwarders and multi-modal transportation workers. Products being transported globally are typically conditional on the Incoterms principles delivered by the International Chamber of Commerce.

Correspondingly to production systems, logistic systems necessitate to appropriately constituted and managed (Bowersox, David & Bixby, 2002). Essentially numerous practices have been openly borrowed from processes administration for example utilizing Economic

Order Quantity models for handling record in the nodes of the network.

Production logistics defines logistic procedures in a production. Production logistics purposes to make sure that every machine and workplace obtains the accurate product in the accurate amount and quality at the correct time. The concern is to rationalize and regulate the movement through value-adding procedures and to eradicate non–value-adding procedures, but not the transportation itself. Therefore, production logistics can function in prevailing in addition to new plants.

Cargo

Cargo is goods or products conveyed, commonly for profitable gain, by boat or airplane, even though the term is currently comprehensive to intermodal train, and truck. In contemporary times, containers get utilized in most long-haul cargo conveyance.

Transportation types

Marine

Automobiles get moved at various ports and get frequently transported through particular roll-off ships. Break bulk cargo is characteristically substances loaded on pallets and elevated on the dock or aboard the ship by cranes (Brandimarte & Zotteri, 2007). Drastically, as containerization has grown, the capacity of break bulk cargo has deteriorated international.

Air

Air cargo, frequently referred to as air freight, is composed of companies from shippers and transported to clienteles. In 1911, aircraft were principally utilized for transporting mailing. Ultimately producers started scheming airplane for other kinds of cargo in addition. There are numerous trade aircraft appropriate for transporting cargo for example the Boeing 747 which was intentionally constructed for easy transformation into a cargo airplane.

Train

Trains are able of conveying big amounts of containers that come from shipments ports. Trains are similarly utilized for the conveyance of heavy products such as steel. They get utilized since they can transport a big quantity and normally have a nonstop track to the terminus. Under the correct conditions, cargo conveyance by train is more cost-effective and energy resourceful than by road, particularly when transported in large amount or over extensive distances.

Road

Many corporations such as Parcel force transport all kinds of goods by road. Transporting everything from mails to households to load containers, these corporations provide fast, occasionally same-day, distribution. An amazing instance of road freight is fruits, as superstores necessitate distributions each day to retain their shelves supplied with products.

Shipment categories

Cargo is typically prearranged into a number of cargo classifications before it gets conveyed. An item's classification gets regulated by: the kind of substance being carried. For instance, a pot could suit into the classification 'household products'.

Cargo airline, Cargo sampling, cargo scanning and delivery

Cargo airlines are air companies devoted to the transport of cargo. Some freight commercial airlines are divisions or affiliates of bigger passenger air companies. Air transport is an important constituent of numerous transnational logistics networks, vital to handling and governing the movement of products, energy, data, services, and people, from one point to the other.

Cargo sampling is the taking and holding of proper illustrative samples of products goods, habitually to enable imbursement to a transporter for shipment leaving its port of stacking. On the other hand, for cargo airlines to be effective they require to do cargo scanning. Cargo scanning or non-intrusive inspection (NII) denotes to non-damaging techniques of examining and recognizing products in transport systems (Brandimarte & Zotteri, 2007). It is frequently utilized for scanning of intermodal cargo conveyance containers.

Freight company, Freight Transport Association, Standard Carrier Alpha Code and Document automation

Freight companies

Freight Companies are corporations that concentrate on the forwarding of cargo, or freight, from one position to the other (Bowersox, David & Bixby, 2002). These corporations get categorized into a number of different sections. For instance, intercontinental freight movers transport merchandises globally from state to state, and local freight movers, transport merchandises within a particular state. There are a number of freight corporations in commerce globally, numerous of which are affiliates of particular organizations such as the International Air Transport Association, Transportation Intermediaries Association, British International Freight Association, and

Freight Transport Association which are among other various regional organizations. Since there are various methods of transportations of goods, some corporations provide multi-modal resolutions; this indicates that they provide more than one deal, in several circumstances air and sea and in other circumstances air, sea, and road (Brandimarte & Zotteri, 2007). Among the various multi-modals, the most common way of transporting is known as inter-modal indicating van pickup to train to truck transport. In choosing the appropriate shipping method, it requires evaluating three factors which are time, cost, and product physical appearance. While transport by sea could consume a lot of time than transporting by air, the latter is in general more costly. Transporting by train could correspondingly be supplemented by ride along the merchandise onto a van so it can get transported to the receiver.

Freight Transport Association

The Freight Transport Association (FTA) got initiated back in the 1889: its duty is to represent the opinions and welfares of over 12,000 corporations: from small corporations and household names to big and medium international businesses. In the UK, it is one of the biggest trade associations with affiliates transporting merchandises by road, rail, sea and air.

Standard Carrier Alpha Code

The Standard Carrier Alpha Code (SCAC) is an exceptional code utilized to recognize conveyance corporations (Bowersox, David & Bixby, 2002). It is characteristically two to four alphabetical letters in length. It got established in the 1960s by the National Motor Freight Traffic Association to aid the shipping industry automate data and accounts.

Document automation

Document automation (similarly referred to as document assembly) is the scheme of structures and workflows that help in the formation of automated documents. These consist of logic-based schemes that utilize subdivisions of pre-prevailing data to draw together a new document. This procedure is progressively utilized in particular businesses to draw together lawful documents, agreements and letters. Document automation systems can as well get utilized to computerize all restricted text, inconstant text, and data contained in a set of documents.

Freight claim, Logistics automation and Performance-based logistics

Freight Claim

A Freight claim is a lawful demand to a carrier by a shipper or consignee for fiscal repayment for a damage or loss of a consignment (Bowersox, David & Bixby, 2002). Freight claims are similarly recognized as shipping claims, cargo claims, transportation claims, or loss and damage claims. The purpose of a cargo claim is for shipper or consignee to be made "whole" by the carrier which makes their situation is as excellent as it would have been if the shipper had done their responsibilities as stated by the Bill of Lading. Thus, claimants are in general projected to file an assertion to recuperate their expenses, not comprising returns, even though in some uncommon circumstances claiming returns may get deliberated suitable.

Claimants are similarly anticipated to take practical actions to lessen the damage. For instance, if the spoiled merchandise has maintained some worth, the carrier would merely get needed to recompense for the variance amid the initial worth and the spoiled worth. The claimant would then be at liberty to recover the spoiled merchandise by vending it at a decreased price.

Logistics automation

Logistics automation is the employment of computer software or computerized mechanism to advance the competence of logistics processes. Characteristically this denotes to processes in a warehouse or distribution center, with comprehensive jobs carried out by supply chain management structures and enterprise supply scheduling systems. Logistics automation systems can strongly supplement the amenities delivered by these advanced level computer systems. The center on a distinct node in a broader logistics network permits systems to be extremely personalized to the necessities of that node.

Performance-based logistics

Performance-Based Logistics (PBL) similarly recognized as Performance Based Contracting or performance based life-cycle product support is a policy for lucrative defense system support. Instead of reaching an agreement for the acquirement of merchandises and services, the merchandise support manager recognizes product support integrator (PSI) to provide execution results as denoted by execution benchmark for a system or merchandise (Rushton, Croucher & Baker, 2010). The integrator frequently obligates to this execution level at a lesser price, or amplified execution at prices comparable to those formerly attained under a non-PBL or transactional collection of merchandise support arrangements for merchandises and services.

Distribution (business) and Agricultural marketing

Distribution

Distribution is the procedure of making a merchandise or service accessible for usage or consumption by an end user or commercial consumer, by means of direct means, or via subsidiary means with intermediaries (Bowersox, David & Bixby, 2002). Among the four components of the marketing mix, Merchandise distribution is one of them with the other three parts of the marketing mix being product, pricing, and promotion.

Distribution of merchandises happens by means of channels. Channels are collections of mutually dependent organizations known as intermediaries included in making the merchandise obtainable for usage. Thus, a corporation can scheme any amount of channels. Channels are categorized by the amount of intermediaries amid manufacturer and end user. However, there a channel that has no intermediaries and this level is a level zero channel which is usually of direct marketing. On the other hand, a level one channel has a sole intermediary and this this flow is characteristically from producer to vender to end user.

In reality, a lot of organizations utilize a mix of dissimilar channels; in specific, they can supplement a direct sales-force who normally appeals to greater clienteles with representatives who cover the minor clienteles and projections. Therefore, the marketing department of the corporation necessitates scheme the most appropriate channels for the company's merchandises, then choosing suitable channel affiliates or intermediaries (Rushton, Croucher & Baker, 2010). The corporation also requires training workers of intermediaries and inspiring the intermediary to vend the company's merchandises. The corporation ought to over time monitor the performance of the channel and amend the channel to improve execution. To inspire intermediaries, the corporation can utilize positive engagements, for instance provide greater margins to the transitional, distinctive deals, dividends and allowances for publicizing or exhibition. Channel skirmish can ascend when actions of one intermediary inhibit another intermediary from attaining their purposes.

Agricultural marketing

Agricultural marketing takes care of the services concerned with moving agricultural merchandise from the plantation to the end user. Numerous interrelated events get included in undertaking this, for example scheduling production, growing and reaping, sorting, packaging, conveyance, storing, agro- and food processing, delivery, publicizing and sale. Some descriptions would also take in "the deeds of purchasing provisions, letting apparatus, (and) disbursing employment", contending that marketing is everything commerce does. Such undertakings cannot happen devoid of the interchange of data and are frequently profoundly reliant on the obtainability of appropriate finance.

All-commodity volume

All-commodity volume or ACV signifies the entire yearly sales capacity of retailers that can get combined from distinct store-level up to greater physical sets. This quantity is a ratio, and so is normally quantified as a one hundredth (Rushton, Croucher & Baker, 2010). The aggregate dollar sales that enter into ACV consist of the complete stock inventory sales, instead of sales for a particular classification of merchandises therefore the term "all commodity volume."

ACV is best correlated to the main marketing idea of distribution. Distribution metrics measure the obtainability of merchandises vended through merchants, typically as a one hundredth of all possible channels. Repeatedly, channels are weighted by their portion of group sales or "all-commodity" sales. Distribution metrics, for marketers who vend via resellers, disclose percentage of market entrance of a brand. Harmonizing a corporation's determinations in "pull" (making client demand) and "push" (building and upholding reseller and distribution sustenance)is a continuing planned apprehension for marketers.

Channel value scheme is a commerce model utilized by dealers to entice affiliates of its distribution channel (Rushton, Croucher & Baker, 2010). This is constituted of numerous components, determined by the complexity of the trader and channel affiliates, and the strength of competition for the channel's share. An extended business is a lightly combined, self-establishing network of companies that conglomerate their financial production to offer merchandises and services contributions to the market. Companies in the extended business can function self-sufficiently, for instance, via market contrivances, or obligingly via treaties and agreements.

Good Distribution Practice (GDP) handles the guiding principle for the appropriate distribution of pharmaceutical merchandises for human usage. GDP is a quality guarantee scheme, which takes account of necessities for procurement, reception, storing and export of drugs envisioned for human usage. GDP controls the partition and transportation of medicinal products from the places of the producer of pharmaceutical merchandises, or another fundamental point, to the consumer, or to an intermediary point through a number of conveyance techniques, by means of a number of storage or health institutions (Rushton, Croucher & Baker, 2010). On the other hand, liquid logistics is an exceptional classification of logistics that links to liquid merchandises, and is utilized comprehensively in the "supply chain for liquids" field.

Import and export

Import

An import is a product taken into a jurisdiction from an exterior source, particularly across a state boundary. The buyer of the imported products is known as an importer. An import in the reception nation is an export from the sending state. Exportation and Importation are the outlining fiscal transactions of intercontinental commerce. In transnational commerce, the importation and exportation of merchandises get restricted by import quotas and obligations from the levies authority. The importing and exporting rules might levy a tariff on the merchandises. As well, the importation and exportation of merchandises are conditional on trade contracts amid the importing and exporting authorities.

There are two fundamental kinds of import: industrial and consumer goods, and intermediate goods and services. This brings about the three broad categories of importers who are categorized by their role in import industry. One kind of importer is one looking for any merchandise around the globe to import and sell. The other one is the one looking for overseas sourcing to get their merchandises at the inexpensive worth. The last category is using overseas sourcing as part of their worldwide supply chain.

Export

The term export indicates transport the merchandises and services outside the port of a nation. The vendor of such merchandises and services gets known as an "exporter" who gets located in the nation of export while the foreign based purchaser gets known as an "importer". In International Trade, "exports" denotes to vending merchandises and services manufactured in the home nation to other markets outside that country.

Export of profitable amounts of merchandises usually necessitates participation of the customs powers in both the nation of export and the nation of import. The introduction of minor commerce over the internet for example through Alibaba has principally sidestepped the participation of Customs in a lot of states due to the low distinct worth of these trades. Nevertheless, these minor exports are still conditional on lawful limitations employed by the nation of export. An import's complement is an export.

Incoterms

The Incoterms guidelines or International Commercial Terms are a chain of pre-defined trade terms put out by the International Chamber of Commerce (ICC) that get extensively utilized in International commercial dealings or procurement procedures (Don, 2013). A chain of three-letter commercial terms connected to common predetermined sales carry out, the Incoterms guidelines get envisioned chiefly to evidently converse the jobs, prices, and risks related to the conveyance and distribution of merchandises.

The Incoterms guidelines are acknowledged by régimes, lawful authorities, and practitioners international for the understanding of utmost frequently utilized terms in worldwide trade (Don, 2013). They get envisioned to decrease or eradicate overall indecisions ascending from diverse understanding of the instructions in dissimilar nations. As such they are habitually assimilated into sales agreements internationally.

First put out in 1936, the Incoterms guidelines have remained occasionally restructured, with the eighth account. "Incoterms" is a listed logo of the ICC and the Incoterms 2010 is the current one which was put out on January 1, 2011(Don, 2013). The eighth put out set of pre-distinct terms, 2010 Incoterms outlines eleven guidelines, decreasing the thirteen utilized in Incoterms 2000 by presenting two novel instructions which are the Delivered at Terminal" and "Delivered at Place") that substitute four guidelines of the previous Incoterms which were the "Delivered at Frontier," "Delivered Ex Ship", "Delivered Ex Quay", and the "Delivered Duty Unpaid". In the previous form, the guidelines got allocated into four groupings, but Incoterms' 2010 11 pre-defined terms get sectioned into two groups founded solitary on technique of distribution (Don,

2013). The bigger set of seven guidelines applies irrespective of the technique of transportation, with the lesser set of four being appropriate solitary to sales that exclusively encompass carriage over water.

In conclusion, it is clear that distribution and logistics are very extensive in supply chain and for them to be successful, the administration of the organization and the team of supply chain management require comprehending all above explained concepts. However, if understood well, they are very important concepts in any commerce.

Questions

1. What is distribution?
   a. Is the procedure of making a product or service accessible for the customer or commercial user who wants it
   b. Is the administration of the movement of products between the point of source and the point of consumption so as to meet necessities of clients or businesses
   c. Is the procedure of making a product or service not accessible for the customer or commercial user who wants it
   d. None of the above

2. What is logistics?
   a. Is the administration of the movement of products between the point of source and the

point of consumption so as to meet necessities of clients or businesses

b. Is the procedure of making a product or service accessible for the customer or commercial user who wants it

c. Is the administration of the movement of products between the point of source and the point of consumption so as not to meet necessities of clients or businesses

d. None of the above

3. For the physical substances, the logistics habitually includes the incorporation of the following apart from?

   a. Information movement

   b. Warehousing

   c. Manufacture

   d. Unpacking

4. The key disciplines of logistics can get subdivided into the following apart from?

   a. procurement logistics
   b. production logistics
   c. distribution logistics
   d. Before-sales logistics

5. Handling systems consist of the following apart from?

   a. Stacker handlers
   b. Trans-pallet handlers
   c. Bilateral handlers
   d. no counterweight handler

6. Which of the following is not a transportation types?

   a. Marine
   b. Air
   c. Road
   d. Gas

7. What are cargo airlines?

    a. Are air companies devoted to the transportation of cargo

    b. Are air companies not devoted to the transportation of cargo

    c. Are road companies devoted to the transportation of cargo

    d. None of the above

8. What is cargo sampling?

    a. Is the taking and holding of proper illustrative samples of products goods, habitually to enable imbursement to a transporter for shipment leaving its port of stacking

    b. Is the taking and holding of inappropriate illustrative samples of products goods, habitually to enable imbursement to a transporter for shipment leaving its port of stacking

c. Is the taking and holding of proper illustrative samples of products goods, unusually to enable imbursement to a transporter for shipment leaving its port of stacking

d. None of the above

9. What is cargo scanning?

   a. Denotes to non-damaging techniques of examining and recognizing products in transport systems

   b. Denotes to damaging techniques of examining and recognizing products in transport systems

   c. Denotes to non-damaging techniques of examining and recognizing products in production

   d. None of the above

10. What are Freight Companies?

    a. Are corporations that do not concentrate on the forwarding of cargo, or freight, from one position to the other

    b. Are corporations that concentrate on the forwarding of cargo, or freight, from one position to the other

    c. Are corporations that concentrate on the receiving of cargo, or freight, from one place

    d. None of the above

11. The Freight Transport Association (FTA) got initiated back in the?

    a. 1889

    b. 2000

    c. 1985

    d. 1970

12. The Standard Carrier Alpha Code (SCAC) is an exceptional code utilized to?

a. Recognize transportation corporations

b. Reject transportation companies

c. Abandon transportation companies

d. Recognize receiving companies

13. The Standard Carrier Alpha Code (SCAC) got established in?

    a. 1980s

    b. 1940s

    c. 1990s

    d. 1960s

14. What is a freight claim?

    a. It is a lawful demand to a carrier by a shipper or consignee for fiscal repayment for a damage or loss of a consignment

    b. It is a unlawful demand to a carrier by a shipper or consignee for fiscal repayment for a damage or loss of a consignment

c. It is a lawful demand to a carrier by a shipper or consignee for non-fiscal repayment for a undamaged or loss of a consignment

d. None of the above

15. What is logistics automation?

    a. Is the lack of employment of computer software or computerized mechanism to advance the competence of logistics processes

    b. Is the employment of computer software or computerized mechanism to advance the competence of logistics processes

    c. Is the employment of computer software or computerized mechanism not to advance the competence of logistics processes

    d. None of the above

16. The Incoterms guidelines was first established in

    a. 1936

b. 1976

c. 1984

d. 1978

17. Distribution of merchandises happens by means of?

    a. Channels

    b. Road

    c. Air

    d. Water

18. What is an import?

    a. Is a product taken into a jurisdiction from an interior source, particularly across a state boundary

b. Is a product taken into a jurisdiction from an exterior source, particularly not across a state boundary

c. Is a person taken into a jurisdiction from an exterior source, particularly across a state boundary

d. None of the above

19. All-commodity volume or ACV signifies?

    a. The entire binary sales capacity of retailers that can get combined from distinct store-level up to greater physical sets

    b. The entire yearly sales capacity of retailers that can get combined from distinct store-level up to greater physical sets

    c. The entire binary sales capacity of buyers that can get combined from distinct store-level up to greater physical sets

    d. None of the above

20. Agricultural marketing take care of the services concerned with?

    a. Moving agricultural merchandise from the plantation to the end user
    b. Moving non-agricultural merchandise from the plantation to the end user
    c. Moving agricultural merchandise from the plantation to the producer
    d. None of the above

References

Bowersox, D. J., David J. C. & Bixby C. M. (2002). *Supply chain logistics management*. New York, NY: McGraw-Hill.

Brandimarte, P. & Zotteri, G. (2007). *Introduction to distribution logistics*. Hoboken, N.J: Wiley-Interscience.

Don B. M. (2013). *International business law : text, cases, and readings (6th ed., international ed.)*. Harlow: Pearson.

Rushton, A., Croucher, P. & Baker, P. (2010). *The handbook of logistics & distribution management (4th ed.)*. London: Kogan Page.

Printed in Great Britain
by Amazon